UNNATURAL DISASTERS

RAVAGED LANDSCAPES

By Sarah Machajewski

Gareth Stevens
PUBLISHING

Please visit our website, www.garethstevens.com. For a free color catalog of all our high-quality books, call toll free 1-800-542-2595 or fax 1-877-542-2596.

Cataloging-in-Publication Data
Names: Machajewski, Sarah.
Title: Ravaged landscapes / Sarah Machajewski.
Description: New York : Gareth Stevens Publishing, 2018. | Series: Unnatural disasters | Includes index.
Identifiers: ISBN 9781538205204 (pbk.) | ISBN 9781538205211 (library bound) | ISBN 9781538205396 (6 pack)
Subjects: LCSH: Natural disasters–Juvenile literature. | Environmental degradation– Juvenile literature.
Classification: LCC GB5019.M33 2018 | DDC 363.34–dc23

First Edition

Published in 2018 by
Gareth Stevens Publishing
111 East 14th Street, Suite 349
New York, NY 10003

Designer: Sam DeMartin
Editor: Joan Stoltman

Photo credits: Cover, p. 1 Tormod Sandtorv/Wikimedia Commons; p. 5 Kyodo News/ Kyodo News/Getty Images; p. 7 (top) Universal History Archive/Universal Images Group/Getty Images; pp. 7 (bottom), 21 (top) Luchenko Yana/Shutterstock.com; p. 9 Vasyl Yosypchuk/Shutterstock.com; p. 10 Bloomberg/Bloomberg/Getty Images; p. 11 Ingo Menhard/Shutterstock.com; p. 13 (bottom) Giles Clarke/Getty Images News/ Getty Images; p. 13 (top) Darkydoors/Shutterstock.com; p. 15 (top) National Nuclear Security Administration/digital version by Science Faction/Getty Images; p. 15 (bottom) The Asahi Shimbun/The Asahi Shimbun/Getty Images; p. 16 UniversalImagesGroup/Universal Images Group/Getty Images; p. 17 dikobraziy/ Shutterstock.com; p. 18 Roberts Vicups/Shutterstock.com; p. 19 (farm animals) Karuiana/Shutterstock.com; p. 19 (power plant) VoodooDot/Shutterstock.com; p. 19 (people) Sapann Design/Shutterstock.com; p. 19 (fish) mallinka/ Shutterstock.com; p. 19 (vegetables) robuart/Shutterstock.com; p. 19 (mountains) VectorShow/Shutterstock.com; p. 21 (bottom) Denton Rumsey/Shutterstock.com; p. 23 (top) Patrick AVENTURIER/Gamma_Rapho/Getty Images; p. 23 (bottom) Barcroft Media/Barcroft Media/Getty Images; pp. 24, 25 mTaira/Shutterstock.com; p. 27 (top) Barbara Davidson/Los Angeles Times/Getty Images; p. 27 (owl) Jim Cumming/Shutterstock.com; p. 29 (top) ESB Professional/Shutterstock.com; p. 29 (bottom) Jacek Chabraszewski/Shutterstock.com.

Printed in China

CPSIA compliance information: Batch #CS17GS: For further information contact Gareth Stevens, New York, New York at 1-800-542-2595.

CONTENTS

Words in the glossary appear in **bold** type
the first time they are used in the text.

WHAT A DISASTER!

Planet Earth is in a state of constant change. Green lands were once covered in ice. Islands have formed from volcanoes. Continents have changed shape. Earthquakes have collapsed land into the ocean. Tall mountains, deep canyons, flat deserts: these landscapes formed over millions of years, giving us spectacular scenery to enjoy. When nature is left alone, the process of change is long and slow. But nature is never left alone anymore. People now populate most of the planet, which has affected every **environment** on Earth. Even places like Antarctica and the ocean floor—where no people live—are affected by people. People haven't been kind to Earth. They've misused its resources, spilled toxins, polluted air, and much more. These unnatural events have changed and even destroyed landscapes for good.

DISASTROUS EVENTS

Scientists put major **disasters** into two categories: natural disasters and man-made disasters. A natural disaster is a naturally occurring event that causes damage or even loss of life. Floods and earthquakes are examples of natural disasters. A man-made disaster is caused by human activity. Leaks, spills, explosions, and other man-made disasters can damage and kill. Man-made disasters are often preventable, which makes their damage all the more devastating, or disastrous, for an affected community.

4

Man-made disasters can quickly devastate an environment and throw an ecosystem out of balance.

LASTING EFFECT

Wind, water, and weather are three forces that naturally form, shape, and change landscapes. Once a landscape is changed, either by nature or man, it's extremely difficult to return it to its original state.

BLACK BLIZZARDS

Beginning in the 1860s, settlers cleared the southern Great Plains to build farms. As millions of acres of land were cleared and flattened, wide-open areas became exposed to extreme weather conditions—especially wind.

Four bad **droughts** hit in the 1930s. Farmland turned dry and dusty, and crops died. Close to 360 separate windstorms created huge, deadly dust storms called "black blizzards." You couldn't go outdoors when these storms raged through parts of Colorado, Kansas, New Mexico, Texas, Nebraska, North and South Dakota, and Oklahoma. The area became known as the Dust Bowl. Farmers were forced to leave their homes and head west in search of land, jobs, and food. They left behind a wasteland of dry dirt where people couldn't breathe, let alone farm, until 1940.

MORE TERRIBLE DUST BOWL FACTS

- over 2.5 million people left the affected states

- centipedes, spiders, crickets, and grasshoppers plagued many areas

- more than 75 percent of America would experience these dust storms, including New York, Atlanta, Washington, DC, and Chicago

- unknown thousands of cattle, sheep, chickens, and wild animals were killed

- blackouts could last 11 hours, dust storms could last 3.5 days

- 100 million acres (40 million ha) of land were destroyed over 10 years

The areas affected by drought couldn't be farmed for an entire decade! Eventually, the rains came again, returning the land to the people. To make sure this never happened again, many farming laws were passed in the years after this unnatural disaster.

DUST BOWL DAMAGES

area with most severe
dust storm damage

other areas damaged by
dust storms

Dust Bowl States

MINING MAKES
A MESS

The Sukinda Valley in India was once one of the top 10 most polluted places in the world. This megamining site isn't on the list anymore, though. It wasn't cleaned, but was instead replaced by even worse polluted places in recent years.

Mining removes natural materials, such as coal and metals, from the earth, but doing so often poisons local people and environments. The Sukinda Valley has one of the largest open mines in the world and has been in operation since 1950.

FAMOUS MINING DISASTERS

Mining gives us important materials we need for building and creating goods. However, mines can quickly kill if an accident or explosion occurs. Some of history's deadliest mining disasters include:

- **1906** An underground fire at the Courrières coal mine in France kills 1,060 to 1,099, including many children.

- **1914** An underground gas explosion at Japan's Mitsubishi Hojyo mine kills 687.

- **1942** An explosion of coal dust at China's Benxihu coal mine kills 1,549.

More than 30 million tons (27 million mt) of leftover poisonous rocks have been dumped all over the local area. Whenever it floods, which is frequently, the water flows over the rocks and carries **heavy metals** and other poisons into the local water supply.

The effects this mining has on the Sukinda Valley people and environment should be causing concern, but these mines make so much money that tougher laws and changes to operations don't happen easily.

Around 60 percent of the Brahmani River, the only water source for local people and animals, is badly poisoned. People are also being exposed to toxins by eating contaminated food, such as vegetables grown in the poisoned dirt or an animal that has heavy metals in its system. Mining also creates toxic dust. That dust eventually settles, coating the soil and falling into surface water, and miners breathe it in while they're working.

All this pollution means the people of the Sukinda Valley, not just the miners, are extremely sick. Almost 2.6 million people, which is about one-quarter of the population, show signs of pollution-related illnesses. Shockingly, about 85 percent of deaths in the area are linked to the pollution.

SUKINDA VALLEY MINES KEY INFORMATION

- **what:** the heavy metal hexavalent chromium is released into the environment during mining

- **when:** 1950 to present

- **where:** Orissa, India, especially the villages within 0.6 mile (1 km) of the mines

- **long-term effects:** plants and animals are poisoned, leading to defects, and species dying out; humans and animals can develop **cancers**, breathing problems, **birth defects**, babies dying before being born, women experiencing problems having children

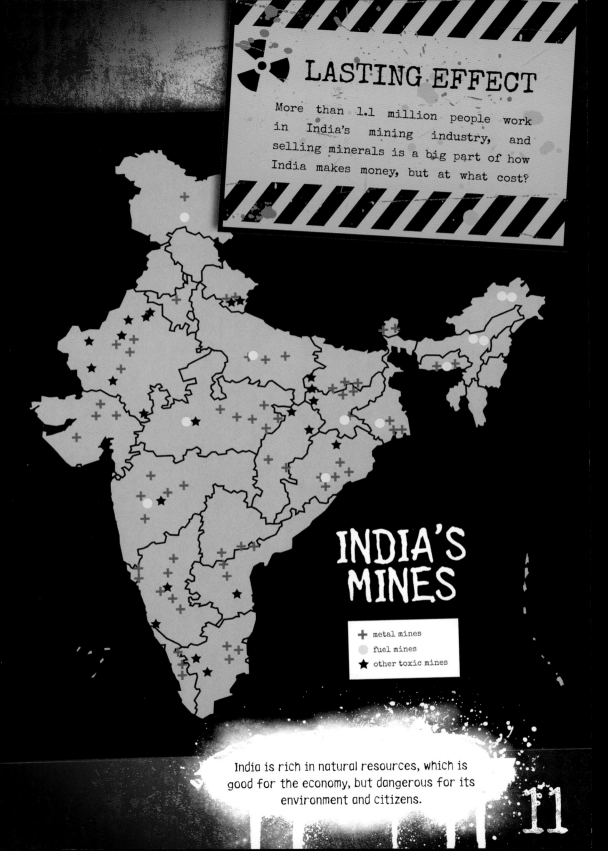

☢ LASTING EFFECT

More than 1.1 million people work in India's mining industry, and selling minerals is a big part of how India makes money, but at what cost?

INDIA'S MINES

- ✚ metal mines
- ● fuel mines
- ★ other toxic mines

India is rich in natural resources, which is good for the economy, but dangerous for its environment and citizens.

THE DARVAZA CRATER: A DOOR TO HELL?

No one knows exactly when or what caused the Darvaza Crater because the local government won't tell. Here's the story many believe: Russian scientists were drilling for oil in Turkmenistan in the 1950s or 1970s. Their drilling equipment was set up atop a huge pocket of natural gas, but it was so heavy it caused the ground to collapse. A 7-story-deep crater formed, as well as a chain of craters across the Turkmenistan desert. Poisonous natural gas and mud spewed out of the crater, and local animals began dropping dead.

How did geologists respond? Light the gas on fire. They thought the natural gas would burn off in a few weeks, but it's still burning today—at least half a century later—and has earned the nickname "Door to Hell."

INSIDE THE DOOR TO HELL

In 2013, explorer George Kourounis entered the crater for 15 minutes. Inside, he was surrounded by deadly gases and thousands of small fires that roared like a jet engine. The edge of the crater was 185°F (85°C). Columns of fire on the crater floor measured 752°F (400°C)! Fire flew out of the ground each time he dug for soil samples. He passed out as his crew pulled him out and barely survived.

one knows how much, nor how much is to feed the fiery crater. Until the gas runs out, Darvaza will keep burning.

The crater is roughly the width of 1.5 football fields and as deep as a 7-story building!

Everywhere you see a flame is an active gas leak!

A CRATER VISIBLE FROM SPACE

TOXIC SNOWFALL

The local residents of the US Marshall Islands, where Operation Castle took place, were never told what was being tested or that it was toxic. After the explosion, news traveled slowly. Many who could have escaped were poisoned. Five hours after the fifth-largest nuclear explosion in history, **radioactive** powder fell on one of the islands, Rongelap **Atoll**. Believing the powder was snow, children ran out to play in it and even ate it.

March 1, 1954, started normally for the US government scientists assigned to Operation Castle. Their job was to create a smaller, lighter **nuclear bomb** to give the US military an advantage in war. After building each bomb, they'd estimate how the explosion would work and then test it—but on this day, they were wrong.

The explosion was about 2.5 times larger than expected. The crater created by the blast is visible from space and is 6,150 feet (1,875 m) wide and 250 feet (76 m) deep! Deadly **radiation** rained down on the environment, poisoning the ground and water. Radiation spread over roughly 7,000 square miles (18,130 sq km), reaching Australia, India, Japan, the United States, and Europe.

The mushroom cloud created by the Operation Castle disaster was 4.5 miles (7.2 km) wide and 130,000 feet (39,000 m) high!

present-day Rongelap Atoll

LASTING EFFECT

The US continued Operation Castle on the Marshall Islands for another 4 years. In total, 67 nuclear bombs were tested there and in nearby parts of the Pacific Ocean between 1946 and 1958.

The 23-man crew of Lucky Dragon No. 5, a Japanese fishing boat 80 miles (129 km) east of the explosion, suffered serious radiation poisoning. One crew member died within days.

The island where this 1954 disaster took place was Bikini Atoll. Bikini residents had been moved to nearby atolls before the disaster, but these turned out to be too close still. Because of the weather conditions that fateful day, Rongelap was one of several islands covered in the deadly powder. Most of the children and many adults on Rongelap at the time would soon develop cancer and serious health issues. Worse, the radiation was in the soil, so it continued to poison the next generation. In all, over 665 residents would suffer from the poisoning.

NO HOME

In 1972, the United States told Bikini residents they could move back home. The island was safe now, they said. Over 100 people returned to Bikini Atoll. But only 6 years later, tests revealed they weren't safe and hadn't been safe that whole time. The people of Bikini were moved yet again. In 1997, an international nuclear organization announced that the Bikini Atoll probably shouldn't ever be lived on again.

The Marshall Islands are far away from most everything, but the radiation of these experiments has traveled all over the world through water. It's still detected in fish off the coast of California!

CHINA

HAWAIIAN ISLANDS (U.S.)

PHILIPPINES

RONGELAP ATOLL

MARSHALL ISLANDS

BIKINI ATOLL

North Pacific Ocean

PAPUA NEW GUINEA

INDONESIA

Indian Ocean

AUSTRALIA

South Pacific Ocean

NEW ZEALAND

Bass Strait

Indian Ocean

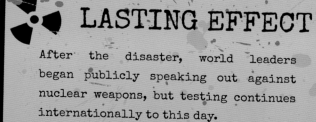

☢ LASTING EFFECT

After the disaster, world leaders began publicly speaking out against nuclear weapons, but testing continues internationally to this day.

A MAJOR WARNING SIGN

Nuclear energy isn't just used for weapons. It's also a power source, though that puts the dangers of explosions, accidents, and radiation closer to homes everywhere. Chernobyl, a town in eastern Europe, was the location of another terrible nuclear power disaster in history.

In April 1986, a series of explosions and fires at the local nuclear power station led to the release of dangerous levels of radiation into the atmosphere. During the following days, wind carried the radiation across Europe and Asia.

The radiation poisoned the soil and water surrounding Chernobyl. People were **evacuated** from the most poisonous area, called an exclusion zone, never to return again. But animals and plants don't follow the rules of evacuations and continue to live there, being poisoned and spreading poison throughout the ecosystem.

People are kept out of the exclusion zone, but animals and plants aren't.

LASTING EFFECT

HOW RADIATION KILLS

Radiation can hurt in two ways: it quickly kills any living thing—from squirrels to daisies to children to trees—if they're exposed to high amounts. Or it kills slowly as its toxic, cell-changing energy is passed through water, food, and air. Radiation slowly builds up in animals and people, causing cancers and other health problems. If radiation isn't cleaned up, plants, soil, water, and people alike will just keep collecting radiation!

HOW RADIATION SPREADS

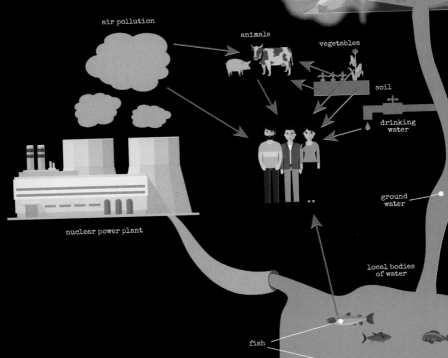

air pollution

animals

vegetables

soil

drinking water

nuclear power plant

ground water

local bodies of water

fish

The landscape was totally toxic after the Chernobyl disaster. The town nearest the nuclear plant was evacuated in the days following, but the radiation traveled hundreds of miles in the air. Many plants, trees, and animals died shortly after the disaster.

After a nuclear disaster, the environment can remain too toxic for centuries because radioactivity breaks down slowly. An exclusion zone is an area declared too toxic for people. But animals and plants don't understand an exclusion zone, so they live inside it. A few scientists are allowed into Chernobyl's exclusion zone to closely watch radiation levels in plants, animals, dirt, and water and to study how the radiation damages and kills slowly. The exclusion zone is a constant reminder of the dangers of nuclear power.

A CLOSER LOOK AT CHERNOBYL

- **when:** April 25 –26, 1986

- **where:** around 77,220 square miles (200,000 sq km) of land in the Ukraine (then part of the Soviet Union) was contaminated; today, 19 miles (30 km) in every direction from the plant is considered toxic

- **short-term effects:** 7 million citizens exposed to radiation

- **long-term effects:** 985,000 cancer deaths; 2 million people still live in heavily contaminated areas, including 500,000 children

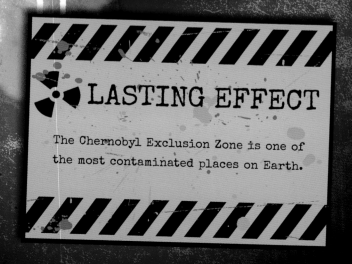

LASTING EFFECT

The Chernobyl Exclusion Zone is one of the most contaminated places on Earth.

NUCLEAR POWER PLANTS
NEAR YOU

Map of the United States with state abbreviations: WA, OR, ID, MT, ND, MN, WI, MI, NY, VT, ME, NH, MA, CT, SD, WY, NE, IA, IL, IN, OH, PA, NJ, DE, MD, DC, WV, VA, NV, UT, CO, KS, MO, KY, NC, CA, AZ, NM, OK, AR, TN, SC, MS, AL, GA, TX, LA, FL

Legend:
- small power plant
- big power plant*

* 2 or more nuclear reactors

Chernobyl didn't stop the use of nuclear power. There are 37 nuclear reactors in the United States that are located within 10 miles (16 km) of 100,000 or more people! A nuclear reactor is the structure that makes the electricity at a nuclear power plant. The energy is created by breaking apart atoms.

A TOTAL MUD PIT

On May 28, 2006, the village of Sidoarjo, Indonesia, buzzed with life and people. On May 29, it was buried under hot mud erupting out of the world's largest and deadliest mud volcano.

Mud volcanoes can occur naturally, but in 2015, scientists were finally able to prove that this mud volcano was caused by a company drilling for natural gas. Most mud volcanoes erupt for a few days, but Sidoarjo's mud volcano hasn't stopping erupting since 2006! As it continues to bury land, the area is beginning to sink into Earth's crust. No one knows for sure what will happen next, when it will stop, or what the sinking will

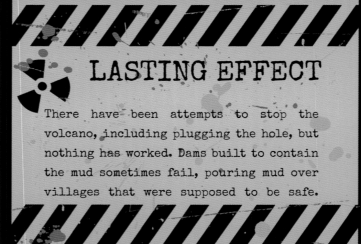

LASTING EFFECT

There have been attempts to stop the volcano, including plugging the hole, but nothing has worked. Dams built to contain the mud sometimes fail, pouring mud over villages that were supposed to be safe.

cause. Some scientists even estimate that the volcano will continue to flow mud for thousands of years!

The residents of Sidoarjo have lost not only homes, but also jobs, businesses, schools, and stores. Their lives and livelihood are locked in a cement of clay and water.

THE SIDOARJO MUD VOLCANO KEY INFORMATION

- **when:** May 29, 2006, to present

- **where:** 2.5 square miles (6.5 sq km) in Sidoarjo, Indonesia, including 8 villages; an area equal to 650 soccer fields is buried in 13-story-high mud

- **how much:** 10 Olympic swimming pools worth of mud spewed daily

- **short-term effects:** 20 people died; 40,000 homes buried

- **long-term effects:** more villages continue to be buried; lung infections; nearby Porong River is polluted with heavy metals

THE DISASTER THAT NEVER ENDS

In 2011, a nuclear power plant in Fukushima, Japan, was the site of a nuclear power disaster that changed its landscape forever, just as in Chernobyl. A tsunami caused by a massive earthquake hit the plant, which hadn't done any recommended safety updates. When natural disaster struck, the plant was badly damaged and released huge amounts of radiation into the environment.

FUKUSHIMA BY THE NUMBERS

- Over 11,500 square miles (29,800 sq km) of Japan is contaminated. An area the size of Connecticut is heavily contaminated. The exclusion zone is over 300 square miles (777 sq km).

- At least 237 million square feet (22 million sq m) of radioactive soil and plant life will need to be cleaned up and stored somewhere.

- No one knows how many animals were affected, but 57 bird species already show major health issues, such as smaller brains.

Today, radiation is still leaking from the plant into the groundwater and ocean, destroying any chances the ecosystem will ever recover. Local marine life and wildlife will continue to be poisoned as long as radiation keeps leaking. Scientists study Chernobyl to this day and have learned a lot about nuclear radiation damage on environments. But there's so much more radiation in Fukushima—and it isn't stopping.

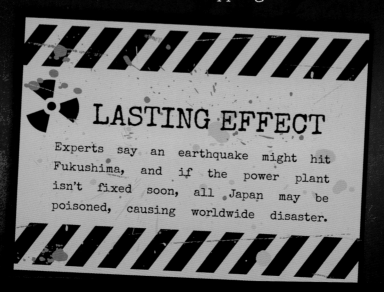

LASTING EFFECT

Experts say an earthquake might hit Fukushima, and if the power plant isn't fixed soon, all Japan may be poisoned, causing worldwide disaster.

A LANDSCAPE ON FIRE

In the summer of 2013, Yosemite National Park placed restrictions, or limits, on starting fires in the park because of the dry conditions of a severe drought. One hunter ignored them. Sparks blew from his campfire and caught the dry landscape around him on fire. It spread quickly and was soon out of control. The Yosemite Rim Fire burned for 9 weeks.

Over 257,000 acres (104,000 ha) of important forest ecosystem burned. That's about the size of San Francisco, California! It destroyed parts of two major forests that are home to two **endangered species** and nine other at-risk species. The fire burned so hot that all plants' seeds were destroyed. The huge number of damaged trees and plants left the area open to the spread of diseases, insects, and weeds, damaging animals' food supplies and home.

LASTING EFFECT

The Yosemite Rim Fire is only the third-largest blaze in California state history. From 2008 to 2013, over 4.5 million acres (1.8 million ha) of California forests have caught fire.

MORE ABOUT THE RIM FIRE

The fire in Yosemite burned five times hotter than boiling water in some places. This high heat changed the soil! It'll take decades to heal the soil so things can grow again. The smoke created from the Rim Fire was as damaging as:

- the smoke, or exhaust, from driving 2.3 million cars

- powering 1.5 million homes with electricity for 1 year

- burning coal at 3.2 coal power plants

Over 75 percent of the area's great gray owl nests were destroyed during the fire!

WE'RE RESPONSIBLE

Countless examples exist of unnatural disasters that have destroyed landscapes and even changed environments forever. These disasters take many forms, but all have people's mistakes in common. Whether it's a miscalculated nuclear test or a toxic waste spill, one thing is clear: our behavior hurts the planet. What else is clear? It has to stop.

It's our responsibility to protect the planet. Earth isn't just our home, but it's also home to millions of plants and animals. Plants, animals, and people need clean air, land, and water to survive. You can help by getting involved with conservation, or caring for the earth. Make your voice heard. Tell everyone, from big companies to your neighbors, they must act in the best interest of our planet. Once our landscapes disappear, they're gone—for good.

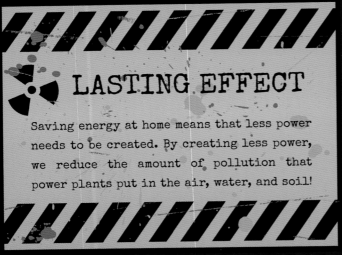

LASTING EFFECT

Saving energy at home means that less power needs to be created. By creating less power, we reduce the amount of pollution that power plants put in the air, water, and soil!

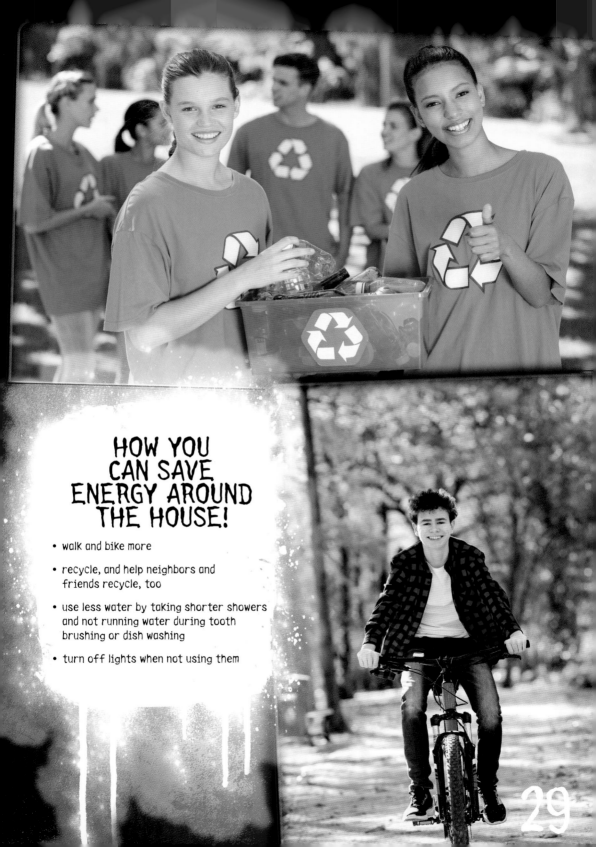

HOW YOU CAN SAVE ENERGY AROUND THE HOUSE!

- walk and bike more

- recycle, and help neighbors and friends recycle, too

- use less water by taking shorter showers and not running water during tooth brushing or dish washing

- turn off lights when not using them

GLOSSARY

atoll: an island that is made of coral and shaped like a ring

birth defect: a physical or chemical problem that exists at birth and is either passed down from the parents or caused by exposure to a toxin

cancer: a disease caused by the uncontrolled growth of cells in the body

disaster: an event that causes much suffering or loss

drought: a long period of very dry weather

endangered species: a kind of animal that is in danger of dying out

environment: the conditions that surround a living thing and affect the way it lives

evacuate: to remove someone from a dangerous place

heavy metal: a type of metal that is very toxic to people and animals

nuclear bomb: a bomb that gets its explosive power from the release of atomic energy

radiation: the process of giving off energy in the form of waves or particles

radioactive: putting out harmful energy in the form of tiny particles

FOR MORE INFORMATION

BOOKS

Black, Vanessa. *Dust Storms*. Minneapolis, MN: Pogo, 2017.

Brown, Don. *The Great American Dust Bowl*. Boston, MA: Houghton Mifflin Harcourt, 2013.

Owings, Lisa. *Pripyat: The Chernobyl Ghost Town*. Minneapolis, MN: Bellwether Media, 2018.

Rissman, Rebecca. *The Chernobyl Disaster*. Minneapolis, MN: ABDO Publishing Company, 2014.

Websites

Chernobyl Children International
chernobyl-international.com/about-chernobyl/
Read all about the children still suffering in the Ukraine and how you can help them!

Disaster Hero: Resource to Get You Prepared
disasterhero.com/resources/kids
Read all about how to be prepared when disaster, natural or man-made, strikes!

The Dust Bowl
american-historama.org/1929-1945-depression-ww2-era/dust-bowl.htm
Read all about the Dust Bowl!

INDEX